Le Corbusier
Shodhan House

Residential Masterpieces 16
Le Corbusier
Shodhan House

Text and edited by Yoshio Futagawa
Photographed by Yukio Futagawa
Art direction: Gan Hosoya

Copyright © 2014 A.D.A. EDITA Tokyo Co., Ltd.
3-12-14 Sendagaya, Shibuya-ku, Tokyo 151-0051, Japan
All rights reserved. No part of this publication may be reproduced,
stored in a retrieval system, or transmitted,
in any form or by any means, electronic, mechanical,
photocopying, recording, or otherwise,
without permission in writing from the publisher.

Copyright of photographs
© 2014 GA photographers

Printed and bound in Japan

ISBN 978-4-87140-641-3 C1352

Residential Masterpieces 16

Le Corbusier

Shodhan House

Ahmedabad, India, 1951-56

Text by Yoshio Futagawa

Photographed by Yukio Futagawa

世界現代住宅全集16
ル・コルビュジエ
ショーダン邸
インド，アーメダバード　1951-56

文・編集：二川由夫

企画・撮影：二川幸夫

ショーダン邸 —「インドのサヴォア邸」—— 二川由夫
Shodhan House — 'Villa Savoye in India' *by Yoshio Futagawa*

第二次大戦を挟んで実施設計にあまり恵まれなかったル・コルビュジエは，戦後，堰を切ったように多くの計画を実現させることとなった。フランスを中心に，ヨーロッパ各地において戦後の新時代に向けた一連の計画は，コルビュジエがそれまでの生涯を通して構築してきた様々な建築的解法の実践の場，集大成となる。戦後の住宅問題については各地に建設された「ユニテ・ダビタシオン計画」(1945年-)がその後のハウジングのプロトタイプとなり，「ロンシャンの礼拝堂」(1950-55年)や「ラ・トゥーレット修道院」(1953-60年)は，民衆の拠り所としての新しい教会建築の地平を切り開くこととなった。

ヨーロッパでの活躍に加えて，老境に入った巨匠は，南北新大陸やアジアでの仕事も手掛けることになる。巨匠の手腕はヨーロッパ文化圏の呪縛を離れ，近代建築の牽引者としての集大成を新天地に花咲かせた。

コルビュジエの手掛けたアジアでの仕事とは，インドにおける公共プロジェクト群と個人クライアントのための秀逸な住宅2軒，日本で実現した美術館であった。植民地支配から解放されて独立した長い歴史を持つ新しい国＝インドでコルビュジエに依頼されたのは，パキスタンとの国境に位置するチャンディガールの新州都の大計画であった。中心となる議場と裁判所を含む新庁舎，および美術館，町全体の都市整備計画は，その後コルビュジエをインドに頻繁に通わせることとなった。これらは1951年に始まるが，ほぼ同時に，アーメダバード市からも美術館（「サンスカル・ケンドラ美術館」，1951-58年)，加えて町の主産業である繊維業組合のための会館（1951-54年）の設計を依頼される。これらの公共建築に加えて，コルビュジエはアーメダバードに2軒の住宅を設計，実現する。繊維業によって財を成した二人のクライアントのための全く異なる建築的解法による住宅は，それぞれ，インドの地に見事にローカライズされた巨匠の代表作となった。マノラマ・サラバイ夫人と二人の息子のための家である「サラバイ邸」(1951-55年)と，元々，繊維織物業協会のパトロンであったスロッタム・フーシーシン氏のために設計されたものの，その後友人であり繊維会社オーナーのシャンバイ・ショーダン氏が引き継いで完成させた「ショーダン邸」(1951-56年)である。この二つの住宅は戦後のコルビュジエの住宅作品の代表的なものであり，同時期，同じ町に建てられたにもかかわらず全く違うアプローチで設計されているのは興味深いことである。この鮮明なコントラストは巨匠の手練手管の表れであり，円熟した建築思考の深さである。

敷地の北西角部からその北辺に沿って豊かな緑の中を進むアプローチ

Although Le Corbusier had few opportunities to fulfill his projects around the time of WWII, he came to bring a torrent of projects into reality after the war. A series of projects for the new post-war era, mainly in France and throughout Europe, became the practicing ground and culmination of diverse architectural solutions that Le Corbusier has developed in the course of his lifetime. The Unité d'Habitation project (1945-), addressing the post-war housing problems and realized in various locations, subsequently turned into a housing prototype, while Chapel Notre Dame du Haut (1950-55) and Convent Sainte Marie de La Tourette (1953-60) opened up a new horizon for church architecture as a an anchor for the public.

In addition to his active career in Europe, the masterly architect in his old age began to work on projects in the New Continents and Asia. Free from the spell of European culture, his mastership found new grounds where it flourished as the culmination of this leader of modern architecture.

Le Corbusier's body of works in Asia consists of a string of public projects, two exquisite residences for private clients in India, and a museum realized in Japan. Commissioned to Le Corbusier in India—a newly born country with a long history that has emerged from colonial rule—proved to be the Master Plan for the new provincial capital Chandigarh located near the Pakistan border. This urban development project for an entire city including a museum and new administration buildings centered around the Parliament building and the Courthouse had Le Corbusier take frequent trips to India. Almost concurrently with this project that started in 1951, the City of Ahmedabad asked him to design a museum (Sanskar Kendra Museum, 1951-58) and a building of the Mill Owners' Association (1951-54) which is the city's main industry. Along with these public buildings Le Corbusier eventually designed and realized two private residences in Ahmedabad. These houses for two clients who made a fortune in the textile industry built with completely different architectural solutions and brilliantly localized to the Indian context became part of the architect's masterpiece: Sarabhai House (1951-55) for Mrs. Manorama Sarabhai and her two sons, and Shodhan House (1951-56) originally conceived for the patron of the Mill Owners' Association Surottam Hutheesing but later taken over and completed by his friend and mill owner Shyambhai Shodhan. Both villas are representative of Le Corbusier's post-war residential works that are, interestingly enough, designed using totally different approaches despite the fact that they were constructed in the same city at around the same time. Such distinct contrast is indicative of the architect's fine mastership and of the depth of a mature architectural thinking.

From the site's northwest corner through the lush greenery along the northern perimeter, the approach leads to the main

を抜けると，「ショーダン邸」のコンクリートのキューブである母屋は出現する。住宅はこの14×15メートル角のフットプリントの五層を収めたキューブと，その北側，植栽に隠れた離れとして渡り廊下で繋がれる一層の建物＝メイドの住まいと台所，ガレージを収めたサービス棟からなる。母屋とサービス棟はともに現場打ちコンクリートの柱梁構造による。母屋の外観で特筆すべきことは，これを囲む4枚のエレベーションがそれぞれ異なる密度の量感をもたらす特徴的な様相を与えられていることである。北東，南東側の開口の少ない面と，南西，北西側のブリーズ・ソレイユに縁取られた開口の多い面は，陽光と気候，全面に広がる外部空間との関係，そして背後に置かれた空間の用途に対して的確に応えている。丹精な幾何学的ヴォリュームは，そこに分割され，それぞれに固有の性格を与えられた内外の空間群によって構成される一つの全体として立ち現れている。この有孔キューブはさらに，頂部に浮かぶように架けられ，フットプリントと同形の大屋根によって一つの純粋幾何学体を完結させている。

ロータリー型の車寄せに面した北東側のファサードは開口部の少ない寡黙なマッスとして建ち上がっている。ファサードは大小2本の水平スリットによって分節が与えられている。上部の開口部はその後ろにある半屋外テラスの大きな空間の奥行きが感じられ，下部の細いスリットには白い曲面壁がファサードに対し彫刻的に配置され，立体感が演出されている。この北東側ファサードの正面左側にはキャノピーが寡黙なコンクリートの壁面から突き出され，静かに訪問者を迎えている。このキャノピーによって光を遮られ，薄暗くなったポーチの奥には玄関である赤色の大扉が浮かび上がっている。

玄関ホールは二層吹き抜けの垂直性の強い空間である。ホール南東側の壁面上部には透明ガラスとともに赤，青，黄の色ガラスの嵌められた窓があり，絵画／彫刻的にフレームを分割，構成する。窓からは刻々と変化する午前中の光がホールの壁と床にハイライトのパターンとして映し出される。ホールはここから始まる住宅内の様々な空間群の前室であり，大扉の正面にはコンクリート製のテーブルと，この建物の主動線である斜路が配置され，これから始まる空間を巡る体験を暗示している。往復し重層する斜路は，建物キューブの南東側ファサードから飛び出すように配置されている。コルビュジエが「ショーダン邸」を「トロピカルな気候におけるサヴォア邸」と称しているように，斜路はこの住宅において重要なエレメントである。斜路は，住み手／訪問者にループ運動をもたらし，その動きが建築の垂直性をダイナミックに表現するとともに，その移動は時間を伴い刻々と変化していく空間体験を与える。斜路に接続する空間群はそれぞれの明るさや，

building, a concrete cube. The villa consists of a 5-level cube with a square 14 m x 15 m footprint, and to the north of it a single-story building connected via a corridor as an annex hidden behind the vegetation housing service facilities such as the servants' dormitory, kitchen and garage. The main building and the service wing are both beam slab structures of cast-in-place concrete. Of special mention on the main building's exterior is that the four elevations surrounding it are each given a distinctive aspect that brings about different senses of density and volume. Northeastern and southeastern sides have less apertures while southwestern and northwestern sides framed with *brise soleil* have many: each one of them responds precisely to sunlight, climate, relationship with external spaces that expand throughout the entire building, and to the use of space that is placed behind. The clean-cut geometric volume emerges as an entirety divided up into a series of internal/external spaces assigned with specific characteristics. This porous cube is complete as a piece of pure geometry, with its main roof that seems to hover above in a shape that follows the footprint.

Facing the rotary driveway is the northeastern facade with less apertures, rising as a reticent mass. The facade is segmentalized by two horizontal slits of different sizes. The upper opening accounts for the sense of depth into the large semi-outdoor terrace behind it, while the thin lower slit is arranged so that a curved white wall is placed against the facade in a sculpturesque manner for a three-dimensional effect. In front of this northeastern facade on the left is a canopy that projects from the reticent concrete wall, quietly welcoming guests in. Light is blocked by this canopy inside the dim porch. Behind it emerges a large red door which is the entrance.

The entrance hall is a double-height space with strong verticality. On the upper part of the hall's southeastern wall is a window glazed with transparent and red/blue/yellow-colored glass panes that divide and layout the frame in picturesque and sculpturesque manners. Morning light through the window changes by the minute and casts highlight patterns onto the hall's wall and floor. The hall is an anteroom preceding to a series of diverse spaces inside the villa. In front of the large door is a concrete table and a ramp that is the building's main line of flow, implying the start of an experience through various spaces. The superimposed half-turn ramp sticks out from the southeastern facade of the cube building. Le Corbusier described Shodhan House as the 'Villa Savoye in a tropical climate'—the ramp is an essential element of this villa. It involves residents/visitors into a loop motion, and while this movement expresses the architecture's verticality in a dynamic manner, the displacement that accompanies time offers an ever-changing spatial experience. Each of the cluster of spaces that connect to the ramp provides an experience that is

ディンメション，プロポーションの変化によって膨張／圧縮された体験を提供する．それはコルビュジエが示唆した，時間と空間の音楽的体験である．往復する斜路を支える白い壁面はこの住宅の室内空間を統合している．壁面に穿たれた有機的な形の二つの孔は，壁面の両側に取り付けられた斜路同士の気配と光を通す．

　玄関のホールから上階に向けて延びる斜路の背後に，居間と食堂の一室空間が広がっている．居間／食堂は二層吹抜けの空間で，一室空間であるものの，その中間部の階高は，書斎であるメザニン階（レベル1 bis）によって低められ，二つの用途の空間はその天井高の変化によって緩やかに分けられている．居間と食堂の南西側は全面開閉ができ，内部空間は，ブリーズ・ソレイユの深い庇によって強い陽射しを避けられるベランダと，その先に広がる広大な芝生の庭，さらに庭の端に位置する大きなプールまで一体化されることになる．居間の南東面と食堂の北西面には，玄関ホールの壁面のもののバリエーションである，絵画／彫刻的にフレームを分割，構成された窓がそれぞれ一対ずつ与えられている．それぞれの窓の，透明ガラスの嵌められたフレームは外部の緑を切り取り，色ガラスの窓は自然光を鮮やかな色彩に変えて室内を飾っている．食堂の背後にはメイドの垂直動線となる階段を備えた配膳室があり，サービス棟の台所と半屋外の渡り廊下で結ばれている．居間／食堂のみならず，諸室内部のコンクリートの柱と梁は打ち放し，それらに縁取られた壁面と天井面は漆喰で仕上げられ，白，赤，青，黄，緑に塗り分けられて華やかな空間となっている．

　玄関ホールから斜路を一往復，つまり1階分を登るとレベル1 bisに到達する．レベル1 bisは南西側に前述の書斎，北東側にゲストルームが配置される．書斎は小空間であるものの，下の居間の大空間を見下ろすことができる開かれたものであり，居間のアクティビティを直接共有でき，さらに南西側の窓からブリーズ・ソレイユに縁取られた緑の庭を見渡すことができる．

　北東側のゲストルームは，居間／食堂，書斎とは対称的に窓の少ないプライベートな性格の部屋で，二層吹抜け，室内に設けられた階段でメザニンとなるロフトレベル（レベル2）のギャラリーにアクセスすることができる．白い曲面壁によって螺旋状に導かれる浴室はドアを介さずに寝室と繋がっている．

　斜路をさらに一層分登ったレベル2には，南北の角部に二つの寝室が置かれている．それぞれの寝室はゲストルームと同様に窓の少ない内向的な空間であり，二層吹抜けの空間である．北角部の寝室には，メザニンとなるギャラリーが設けられている．ギャラリーにはガラス壁が与えられ，その十分な陽光の間接光が下階の寝室に色彩の与えら

inflated/compressed according to the changes of its proportion, dimension and brightness. This is what Le Corbusier suggested as a musical experience of time and space. The white wall supporting the half-turn ramp unifies this villa's interior space. Two organic-shaped holes on the wall let through light and the feeling of presence between the ramps on both sides of the wall.

Behind the ramp that stretches upward from the entrance hall to the higher floors is an expansive open-plan living/dining area. The dining section is a double-height space, and despite the fact that the room has an open plan the floor height of its middle area is lowered by the mezzanine floor (level 1 bis) accommodating the study. The two-purpose space is loosely divided by the change of ceiling height. The southwestern side of living/dining room can be fully open, allowing to integrate its interior space with the terrace under the *brise soleil*'s deep eaves that block intense sunlight, the expansive lawn garden beyond, and the large swimming pool located at the end of the garden. On the southeastern and northwestern sides of the living area are a pair each of windows with frames divided in a picturesque/sculpturesque layout as a variation of that on the entrance hall wall. Each window's frame fit with transparent glass pane introduces the outside greenery, whereas the colored glass frame decorates the interior by tinting the natural light with bright colors. Behind the dining area is the pantry with staircase that becomes the servants' vertical access, connected to the kitchen in the service wing through a semi-outdoor corridor. Not only the living/dining room but other rooms also feature pillars and beams of exposed concrete on the inside that frame the wall and that are plaster-finished and painted either white, red, blue, yellow or green, creating a colorful space.

Level 1 bis can be reached by climbing the ramp half a turn, that is, up one floor from the entrance hall, and houses on the southwestern side the aforementioned study and a guest room on the northeastern side. In spite of its small size, the study is an open space overlooking the spacious living area from where one can directly share the activities that take place in the living as well as have a view of the green of the garden framed by the *brise soleil*.

A room with a private character, the double-height guest room on the northeastern side has fewer windows in contrast to the living/dining room and the study, and has access to the gallery in the mezzanine loft (level 2) through the stairs inside the room. The curved white wall spirals and leads to the bathroom which is connected to the bedroom without a door.

A further floor up the ramp on level 2 are two bedrooms on the southern and northern corners, both double in height and introvert in character with few windows like the guest room. The one on the northern corner comes with a mezzanine

れた天井を反射してもたらされる。
　二つの寝室に挟まれた西角部はテラスが配置される。テラスはこの上三層にわたり展開され，この住宅の第二の居間とも言うべき主要な空間である。三つのテラスはレベル毎にその位置をシフトしながら異なる性格を持つ空間となり，階段によって繋がれた全体として一つの豊かなシークエンスをつくり出している。元々，この住宅の最初の依頼者であったフーシーシン氏が，コルビュジエに求めた社交の場＝パーティ・スペースへの応えがこの屋根付きの三層テラスであった。「繊維織物業協会会館」で用いられた様々なイベントに使われる，自由度の高くこの地の気候に基づいた半屋外の空間のアイディアを，ここで住宅のスケールに翻訳している。この三層テラスには玄関ホールから斜路によって直接アクセスすることができ，下階のプライベートな居間や寝室と分離できるようになっている。テラスはコンクリートの造り付けのベンチやテーブルが所々に配置され，住み手やゲストがこの半屋外空間を楽しむように設えられている。レベル2bisからレベル3へ続く階段はヴォイドの中を飛ぶように架けられ，空間の移動をダイナミックなジェスチャーとしてみせている。大屋根に開けられたスカイライトからは，強いインドの陽光が刻々と動くアクセントをテラスに刻んでいる。

　テラスの最上階，レベル3にはオーガニックな曲面壁に囲まれた水タンクとその廻りを登って屋上テラスにアクセスする階段が置かれる。屋上テラスは白いモザイクタイルに覆われ，下の屋根付きテラスとは全く違う開放感と眺望のある場となっている。

「ショーダン邸」は同時期，同じ町に建てられた「サラバイ邸」と並べられて評される宿命を持っている。一見全く違う住宅であるが，インド独特の厳しく，そして美しい自然環境に対する視線のベクトルは同じ方向を向いている。
　「サラバイ邸」が大地に沿って建つことで，環境と直接的に向き合い融合しようとしているのに対して，「ショーダン邸」は垂直方向につくられる多様で豊かな空間のシークエンスにより，濾過して取り込まれる外界の環境と距離感を持って付き合うための空間装置であるといえよう。「ショーダン邸」は，インドとヨーロッパの自然環境に対する哲学の共振点にある，「インドのサヴォア邸」なのである。

gallery which features a glass wall providing ample indirect daylight that shines on the colored ceiling of the bedroom below.

　The western end between the two bedrooms is the terrace. Unfolding on three floors, the terrace is a key space that shall be recognized as the second living room of this villa. Three terraces on different levels have shifted positions from each other. They are spaces with different characters that are linked through stairs that create a rich sequence as a whole. This triple-height roofed terrace was in fact Le Corbusier's answer to a request by the original client Hutheesing for a place for social occasions—a party space. Here, the idea of a highly flexible semi-outdoor space based on the local climate that caters to a variety of events that was devised for the Mill Owners' Association Building was interpreted into a residential scale. The triple-tiered terrace can be directly accessed from the entrance hall via the ramp and be separated from the private living area and bedrooms on lower floors. Built-in concrete benches and tables are set in places on the terrace, ready for residents and guests to enjoy this semi-outdoor space. The stairway from level 2 bis to level 3 strides across the void, expressing the movement in space in a dynamic gesture. From the skylight opened in the main roof falls the intense Indian sunlight that adds an accent to the terrace as hours go by.

　On the uppermost terrace, level 3, are a water tank enclosed in an organically curved wall and a set off stairs that climbs around it to access the rooftop terrace. Tiled in white mosaic, the latter features a view and open feeling that is completely different from the roofed terrace below.

Shodhan House's fate is to be compared with Sarabhai House, as both were built around the same time in the same city. Utterly different at first glance, both share the same attention directed to the harsh and beautiful natural environment typical of India.
　While Sarabhai House is built in keeping with the ground in an attempt to directly address the environment for fusion, Shodhan House may be described as a spatial device for enjoying, with a certain sense of distance, company with a filtered external environment that is achieved through a vertical sequence of rich, diverse spaces. Placing itself at a resonance point between Indian and European environmental philosophies, Shodhan House is 'an Indian Villa Savoye'.

English translation by Lisa Tani

View from northeast. Main wing (left) and service wing (right)

View toward entrance

Entrance

Entrance porch. View toward service wing

1 ENTRANCE
2 ENTRANCE HALL
3 COATS
4 RAMP
5 LIVING ROOM
6 DINING ROOM
7 PANTRY
8 VERANDA
9 KITCHEN
10 HOUSE KEEPER'S ROOM
11 BATHROOM
12 GARAGE
13 GUEST ROOM
14 DRESSING/BATHROOM
15 VOID
16 STUDY
17 BEDROOM
18 GALLERY
19 TERRACE
20 WATER TANK

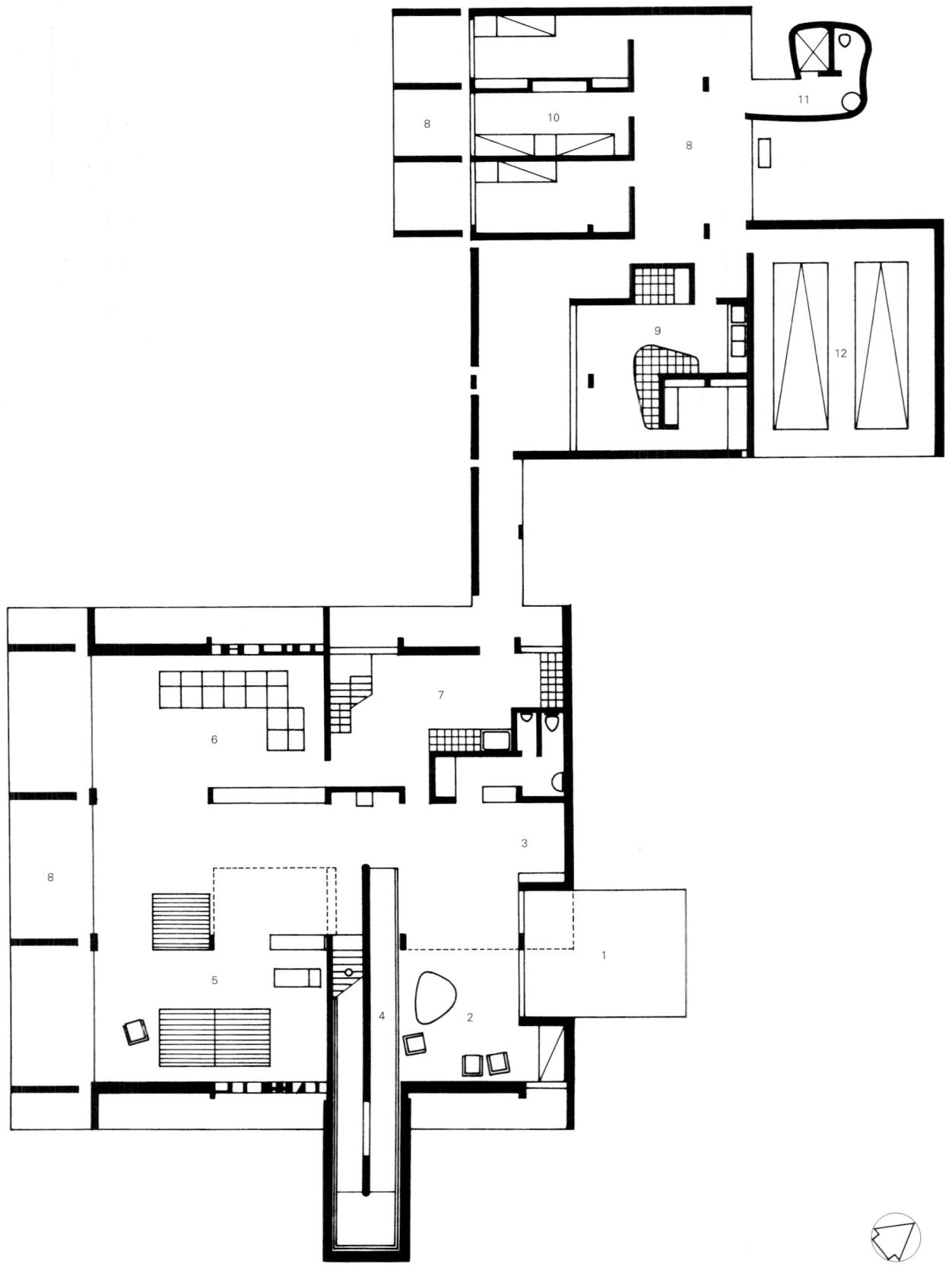

Level 1 (ground floor)

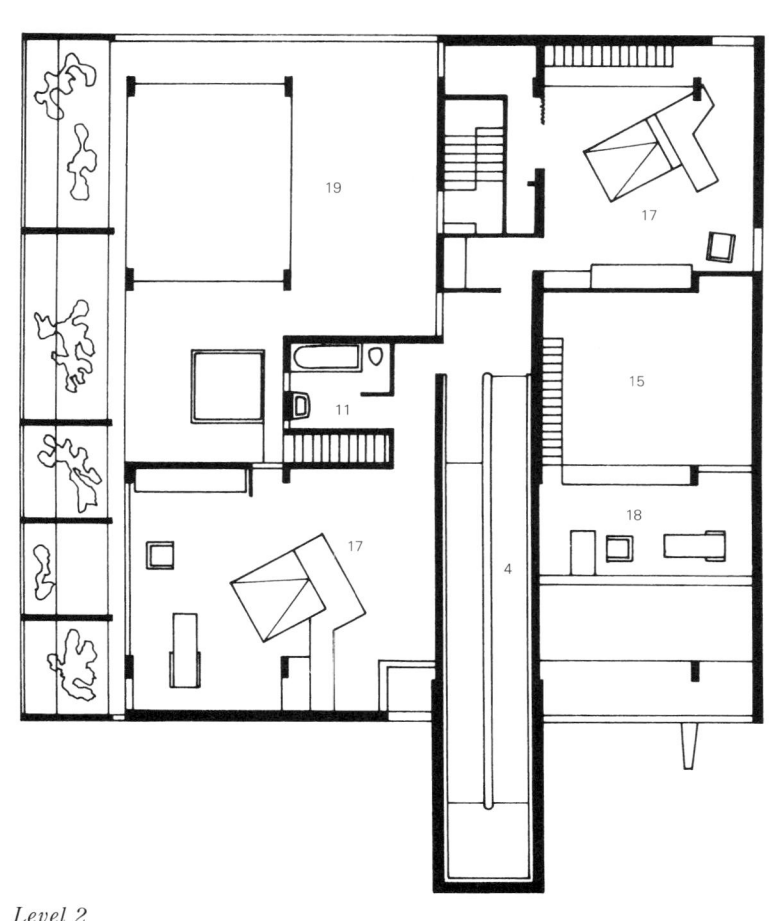

Level 2

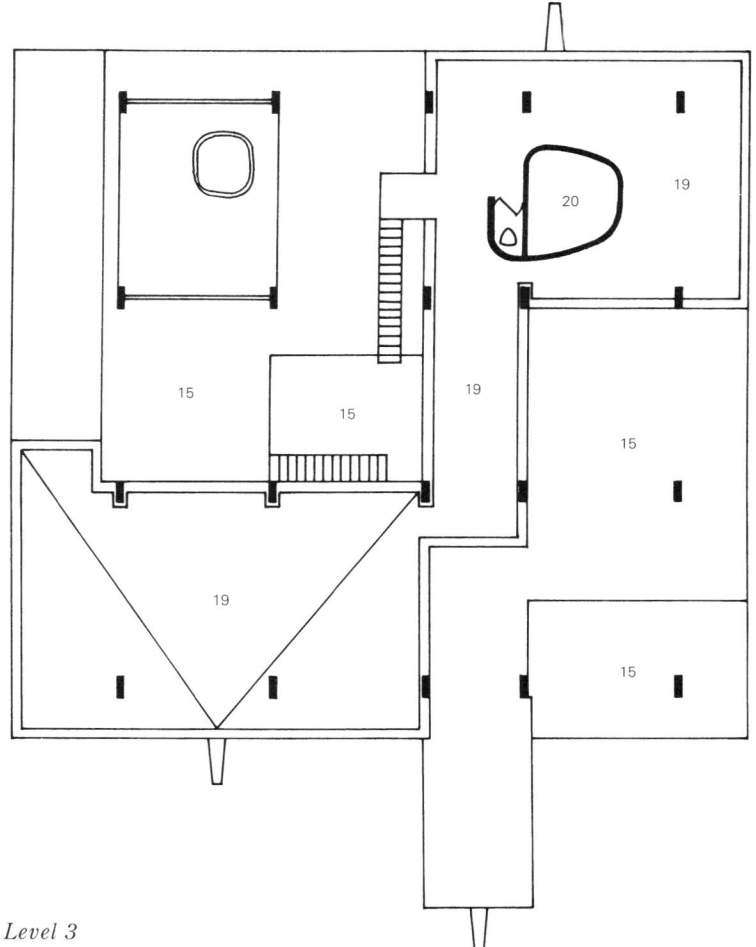

Level 3

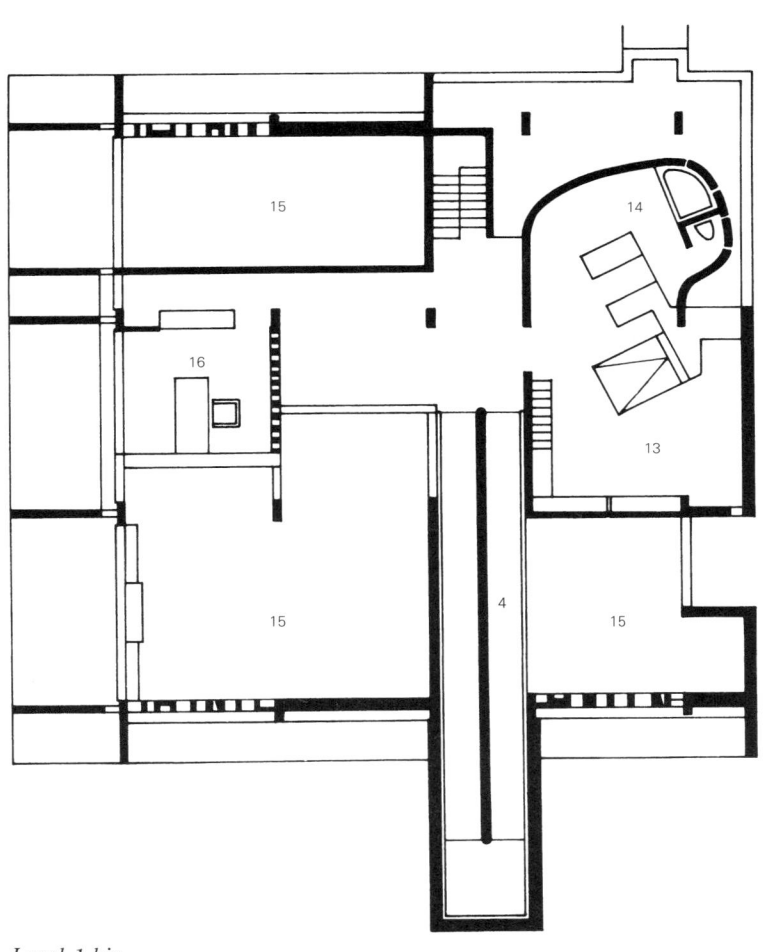

Level 1 bis

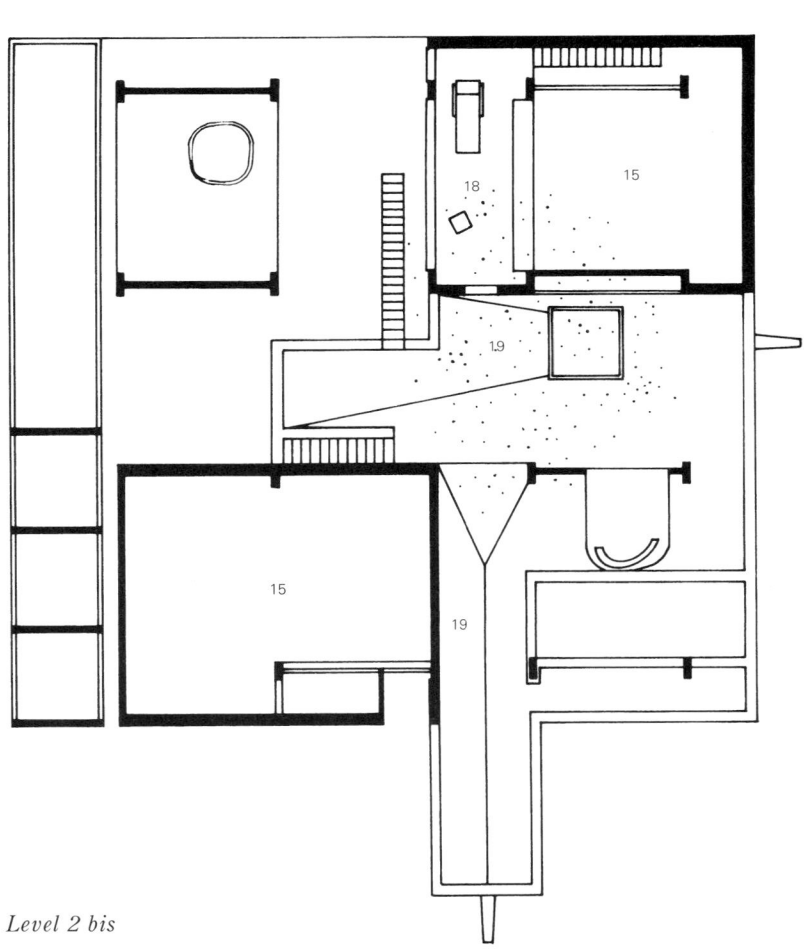

Level 2 bis

View from southeast

View from swimming pool in garden on southwest

View from west

Garden: view from west

Lighting fixture designed by architect

Wall detail on northwest

Wall detail on southwest

Southwest elevation

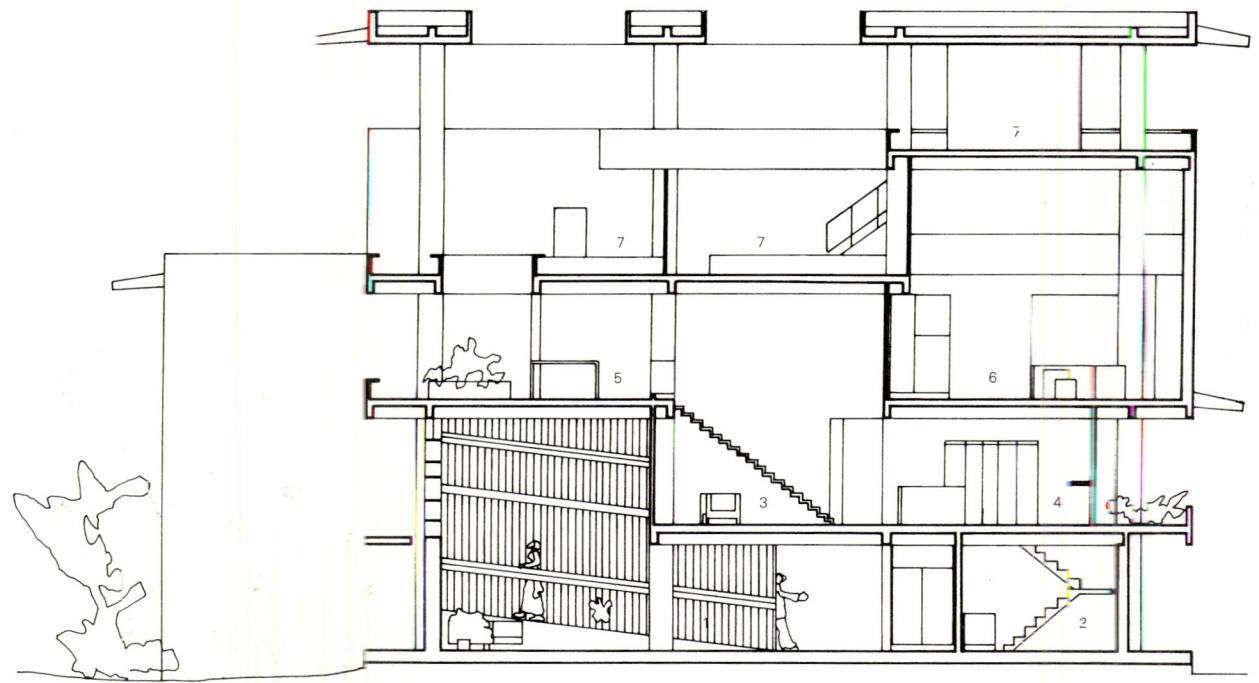

Section southeast—northwest

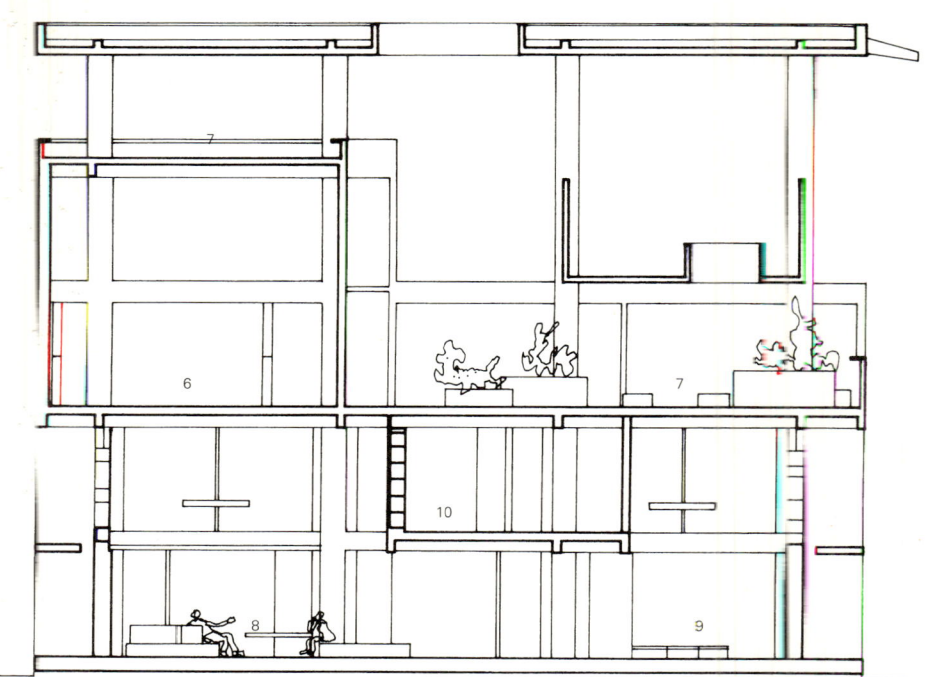

Section northwest—southeast

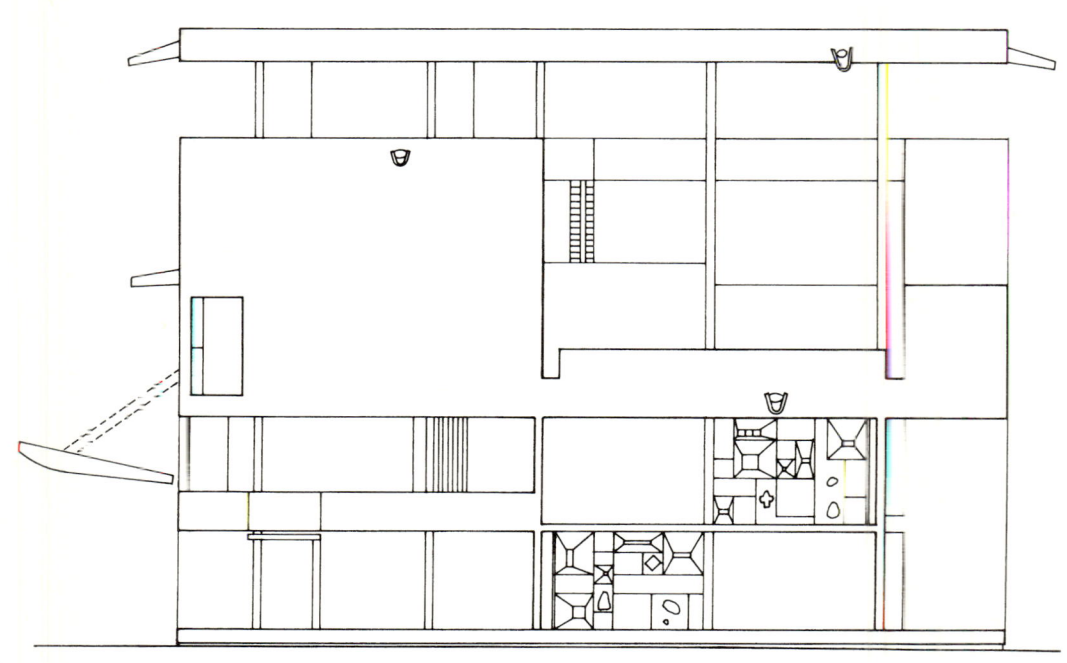

Northwest elevation

1	ENTRANCE HALL WITH RAMP
2	PANTRY
3	GUEST ROOM
4	DRESSING/BATHROOM
5	GALLERY
6	BEDROOM
7	TERRACE
8	LIVING ROOM
9	DINING ROOM
10	STUDY
11	CELLER

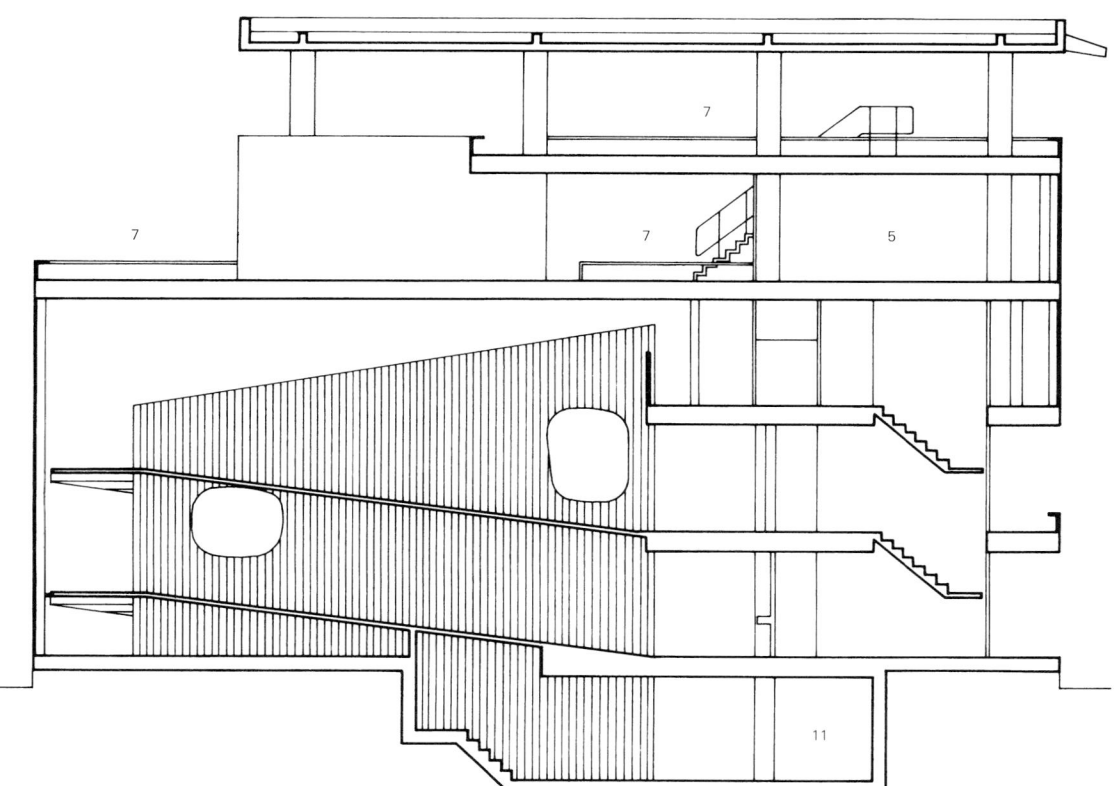

Section southeast—northwest

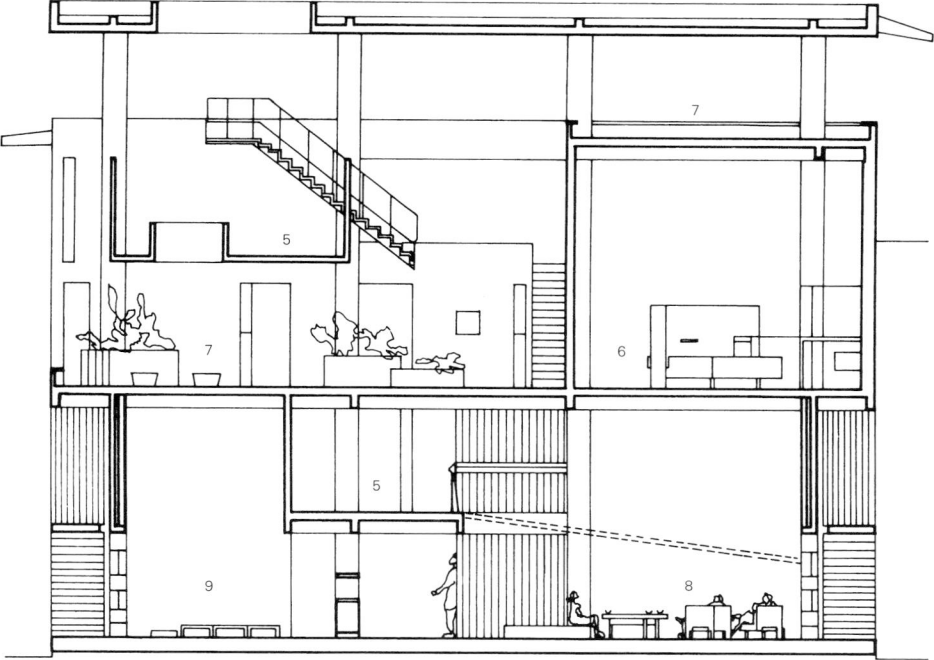

Section northwest—southeast

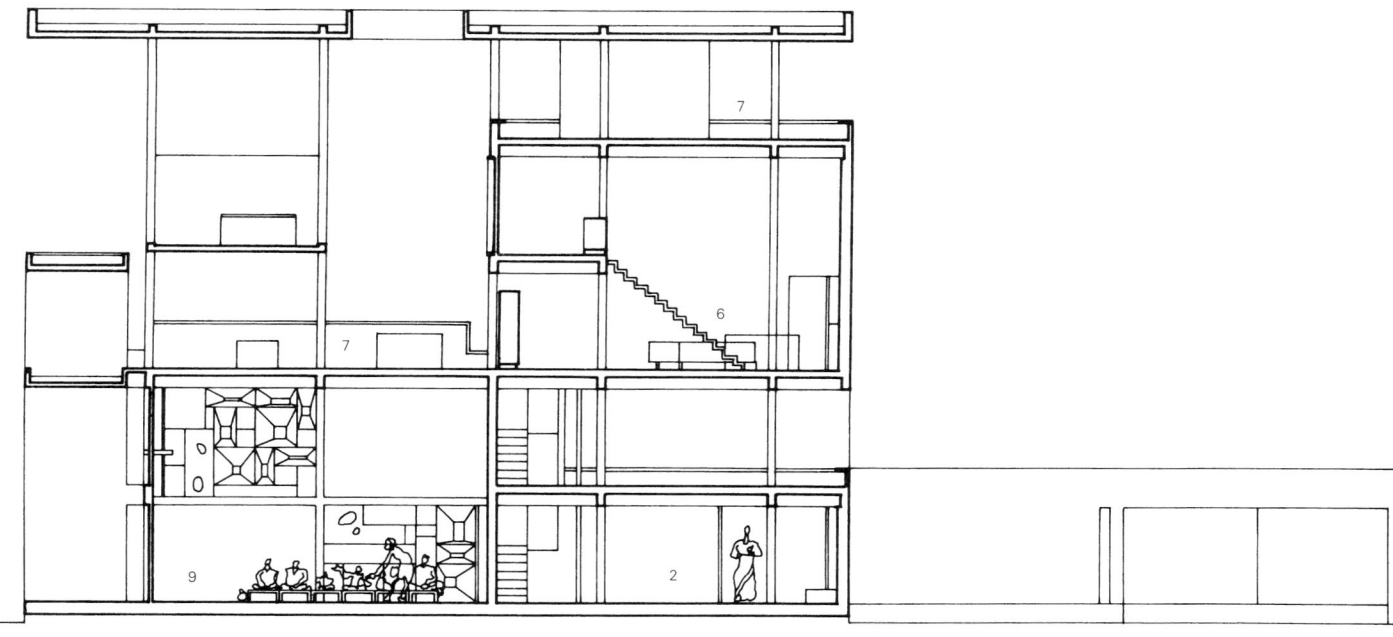

Section southwest—northeast

Entrance

Entrance hall

Entrance hall

Window with openings at entrance hall

View from entrance hall toward living room

Living room

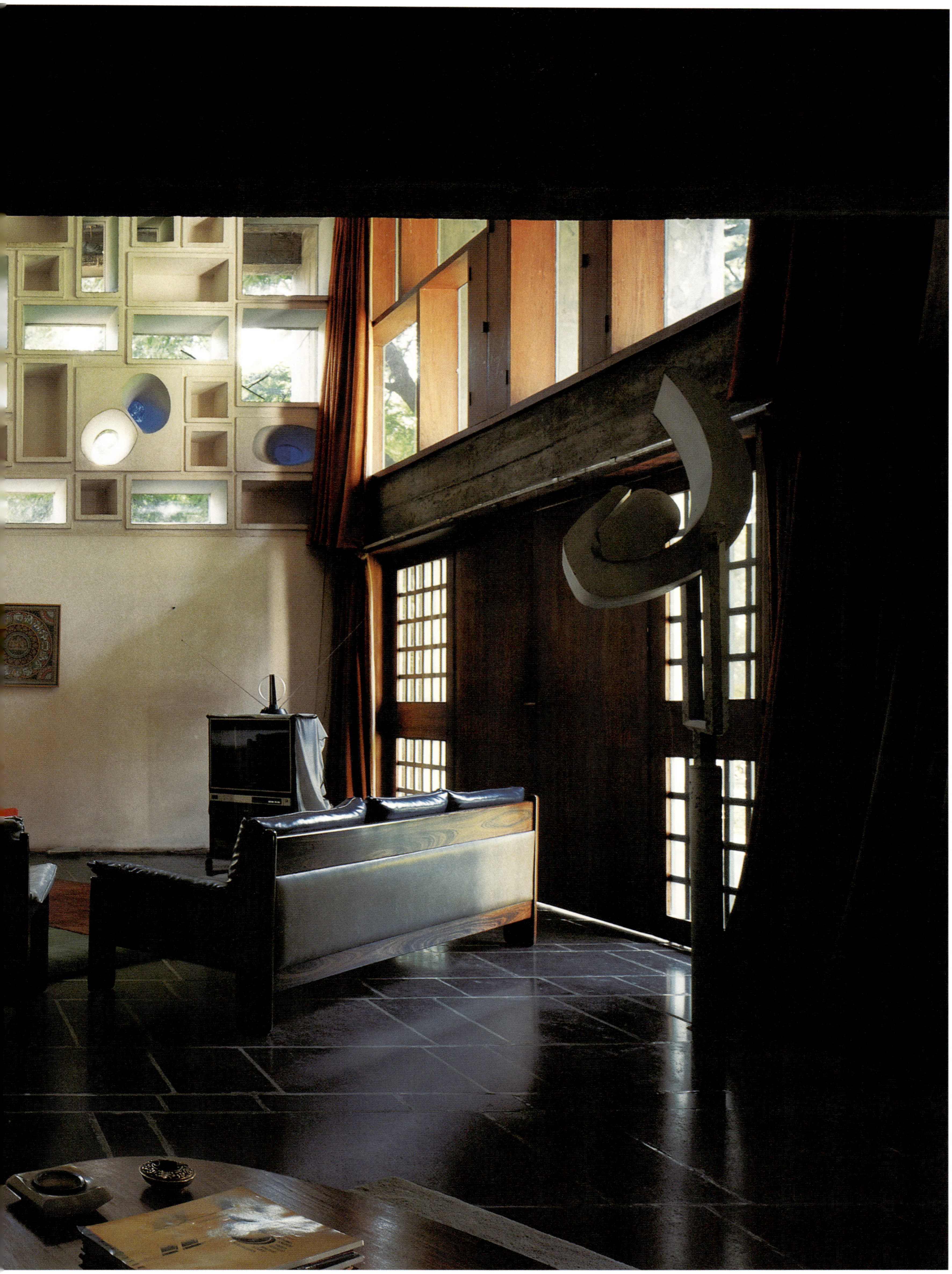

Living room. View toward dining room, study above

39

Living room. Study above

Lighting fixture designed by architect

Dining room

Dining room

Corridor from pantry to kitchen

Kitchen

View of ramp from entrance

Ramp. View from level 1 bis

Ramp. Entrance hall on right below

Ramp between level 1 bis and level 2

Window at ramp

Downward view of living room from study on level 1 bis

Level 1 bis. Study on right

Study on level 1 bis

Guest room on level 1 bis

Guest room. View toward dressing/bathroom

Stairs at guest room. Gallery above

Bathroom of guest room

Bedroom at north corner on level 2. Stairs to gallery on level 2 bis

Bedroom at south corner on level 2

Terrace on level 2. View toward northeast

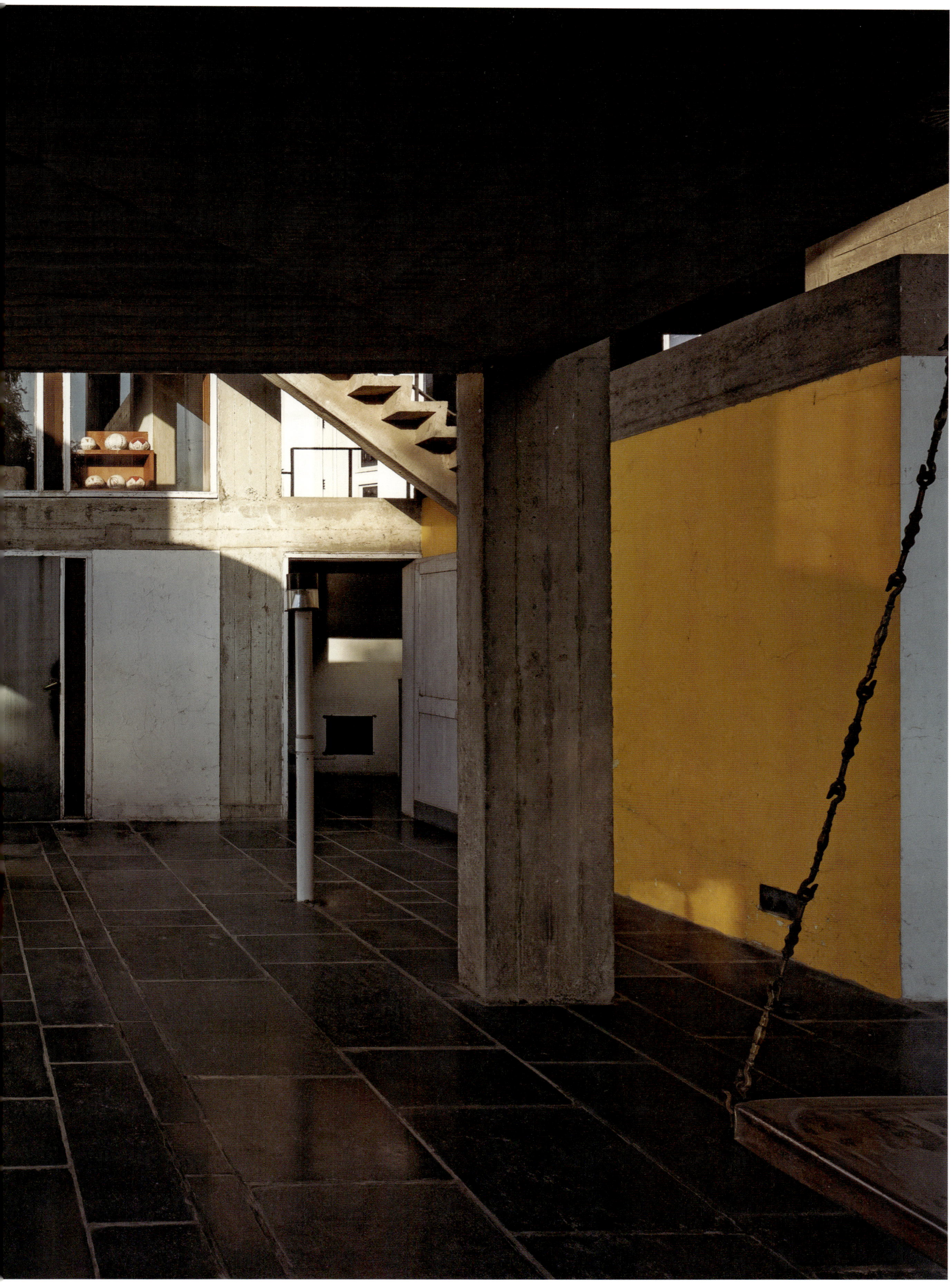

Terrace on level 2. View toward garden on southwest

Bench at terrace

Terrace

Terrace on level 2 bis. Stairs to level 3

Triple height terrace. View toward stairs between level 2 bis and level 3

Projected terrace above ramp on southeast. Concrete bench and table

Terrace on level 3

View toward garden from terrace on level 3

Downward view of terrace

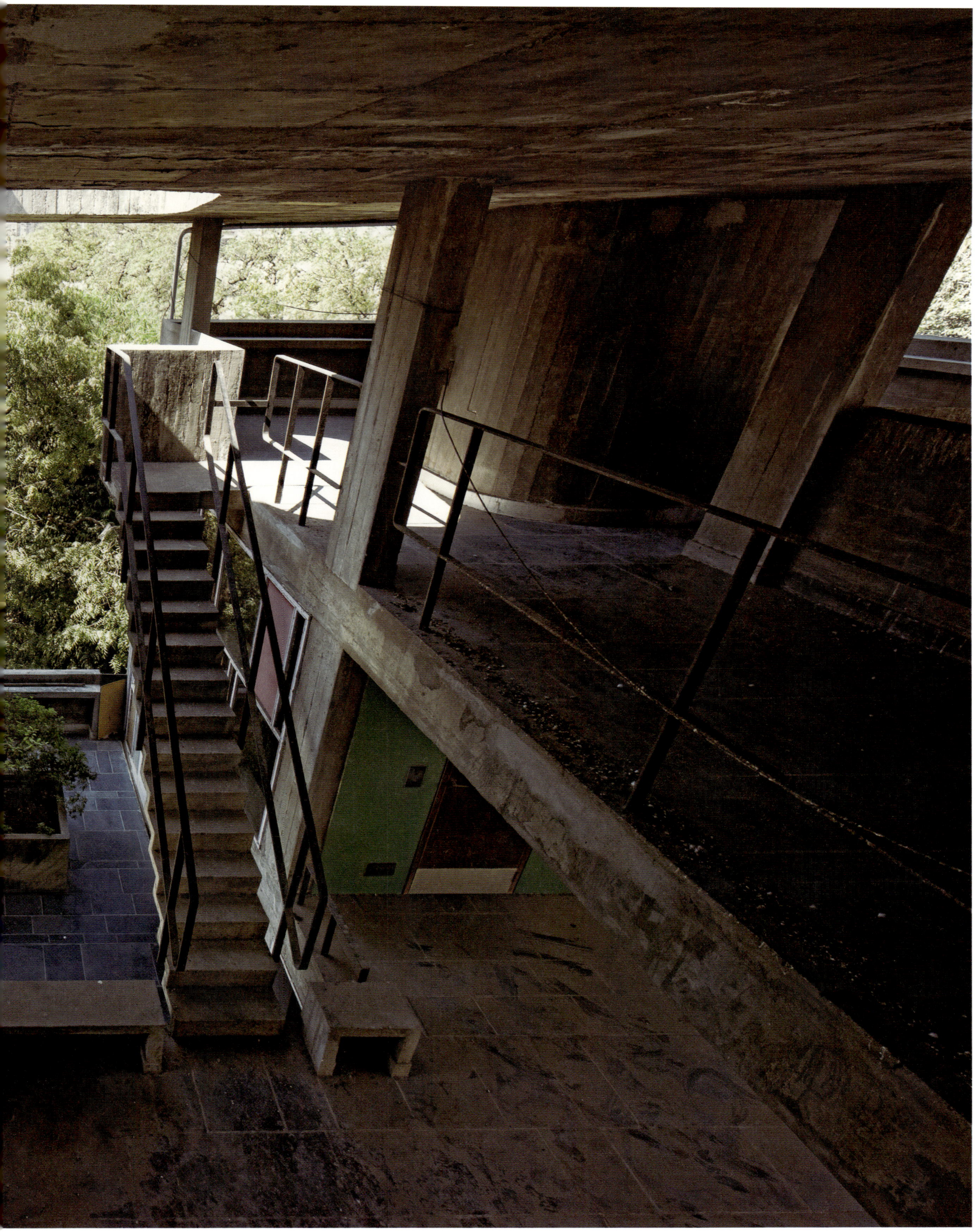

Sunlight through opening in roof

Upward view of opening

Stairs to roof level

Roof level

Stairs to level 3

D.R. (pp.16-17, pp.20-31)

世界現代住宅全集16
ル・コルビュジエ
ショーダン邸

2014年4月25日発行
文・編集：二川正夫
企画・撮影：二川幸夫
アート・ディレクション：細谷巖

印刷・製本：大日本印刷株式会社
制作・発行：エーディーエー・エディタ・トーキョー
151-0051　東京都渋谷区千駄ヶ谷3-12-14
TEL. (03) 3403-1581 (代)

禁無断転載
ISBN 978-4-87140-641-3 C1352